TEARS FOR FEARS

JO-ANN GREENE

BOBCAT BOOKS

London/New York/Sydney/Cologne

© 1985 Bobcat Books
(A division of Book Sales Limited)
Edited by Chris Charlesworth
Art directed by Mike Bell
Book designed by Mainartery
Picture research by Valerie Boyd
Typeset by TPP Limited
Printed by Blantyre Printing &
Binding Limited, Blantyre,
Glasgow

ISBN: 0.7119.0769.2
Order No: OP 43520

Exclusive Distributors:
Book Sales Limited
78 Newman Street,
London W1P 3LA, UK.
Omnibus Press
GPO Box 3304, Sydney,
NSW 2001,
Australia.
Cherry Lane Books
PO Box 430,
Port Chester, NY 10573,
USA.

To the Music Trade only:
Music Sales Limited
78 Newman Street,
London W1P 3LA, UK.

Picture credits:
London Features International Ltd.
Steve Rapport, Barry Plummer,
Virginia Turbett, Chris Craymer

TEARS FOR FEARS

1985 was but halfway done, but Tears For Fears had somehow packed more into those first six months than most bands manage in a life time. A number one single in America, major hits around the rest of the world. A chart-topping LP and concerts which needed only to be hinted at before queues began forming outside ticket agencies. From a reasonably successful act whose string of British hits more than belied their near-anonymity in the media marketplace, Curt Smith and Roland Orzabel de la Quintana suddenly erupted into the very forefront of the public eye. Yet, while – in retrospect at least – this magnificent flowering had always been on the cards, the road to success has been a long one, and one for which, at the start of their career, the duo must often have felt they had missed the turning.

At school in Bath, England, Curt (born June 24, 1961) and Roland (born August 22, 1961) first met in 1974. According to legend, Roland heard Curt singing along to "Then Came The Last Days Of May" – a cut from the first LP by Blue Oyster Cult – and immediately recruited him into one of the several Heavy Metal bands he was leading at the time. Even today Curt has been known to admit "The reason I'm in music now is purely due to the Blue Oyster Cult". For his part, Roland had been playing guitar since he was 9 and had formed his first group before he was even into his teens. The second of three brothers, Roland hailed from Portsmouth. His father was French, his mother Basque-Spanish and his grandfather an Argentinian who was involved in the overthrowing of dictator Juan Peron in 1974. There is a place out in the Argentinian pampas, José de la Quintana, which was named after Roland's great-grandfather.

Portsmouth was certainly a less romantic settlement than that, but it did at least allow Roland his first real introduction to music. His parents ran an entertainment agency from their council home and Roland grew up surrounded by musicians – and philosophers. His father founded the Portsmouth Philosophical Society.

Like Roland, Curt also grew up on a council estate, in Bath. It was, he says, "the most hideous council estate you could ever imagine". And to add insult to injury, he swiftly acquired a reputation as the local punchbag. "I used to get picked on at school because I was small, and the worst thing was that my older brother was even weaker than me, so he was no use!"

Having met, Curt and Roland remained friends – and musical collaborators – throughout the rest of the 1970s, their projects becoming ever more ambitious right up until the end of 1979 when, inspired by the Mod revival then sweeping the country, the pair formed Graduate. Roland and Curt both sang, together with guitarist John Baker. The rest of the band's line-up included keyboard/flautist Steve Buck and drummer Andy Marsden.

Hard working around the local, Bath, circuit, then gaining national exposure when they toured as support to Judie Tzuke (herself riding high in the chart with her "Sports Car" album), Graduate signed to the PRT/Precision label at the beginning of 1980. Straight away they found themselves with some chart success; "Elvis Should Play Ska", their début single, reached number 106 in England. And while Graduate were never to follow up even that minor victory in their home country, they did accrue something of a following in

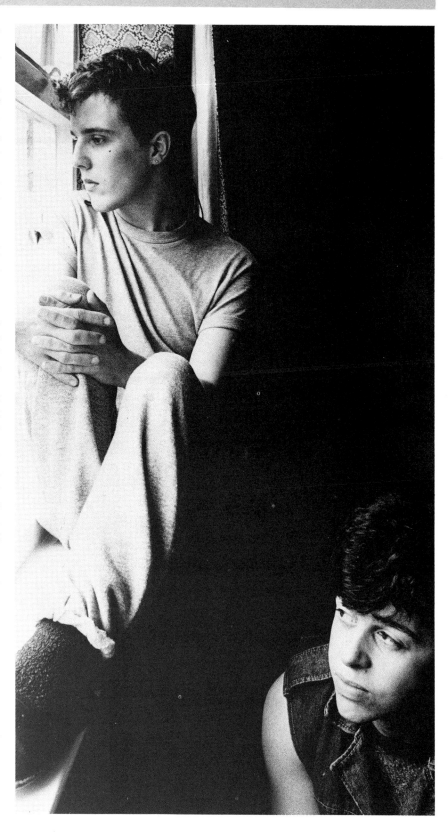

Spain and the group's next three singles were all sizeable hits in Roland's maternal homeland. They were even to release an LP: in May, 1980, "Acting My Age" was released to few reviews and even fewer sales. Not surprisingly, Graduate is an episode which Roland and Curt would be quite happy to forget.

"The thing with Graduate is that basically we were rubbish and we didn't know what we were doing," Roland told Ireland's *Hot Press* late in 1981. "We spent two years doing Graduate and it got us nowhere. We did tours of Germany, Spain and that sort of thing and it was endless. The other guys believed that hard work paid off in the end, but it doesn't if the product isn't there. We were just totally wrong in everything we did. It was terrible – I cringe listening to what we did." More succinctly, he told *Melody Maker's* Steve Sutherland: "Graduate were a crap sort of rubbish pop group." None of which has stopped that group's records from attaining a near-legendary status amongst record collectors; one magazine recently valued "Acting My Age" at £10!

Graduate broke up midway through 1981, unnoticed and unmourned, and Roland and Curt immediately put their minds towards forming a new band. Although they had stuck with Graduate for approaching two years, they were both well aware that riding (or attempting to ride) to fame on the shirt sleeves of the latest pop fashion, as Graduate had so patently been trying to do, was no way to achieve any lasting satisfaction. And even though, towards the end of their career, the group had shown strong signs of developing into something far more lasting than the novelty-ska beat of their "Elvis" single ever indicated, both boys realised that the only way they could achieve their aims would be to make a fresh start.

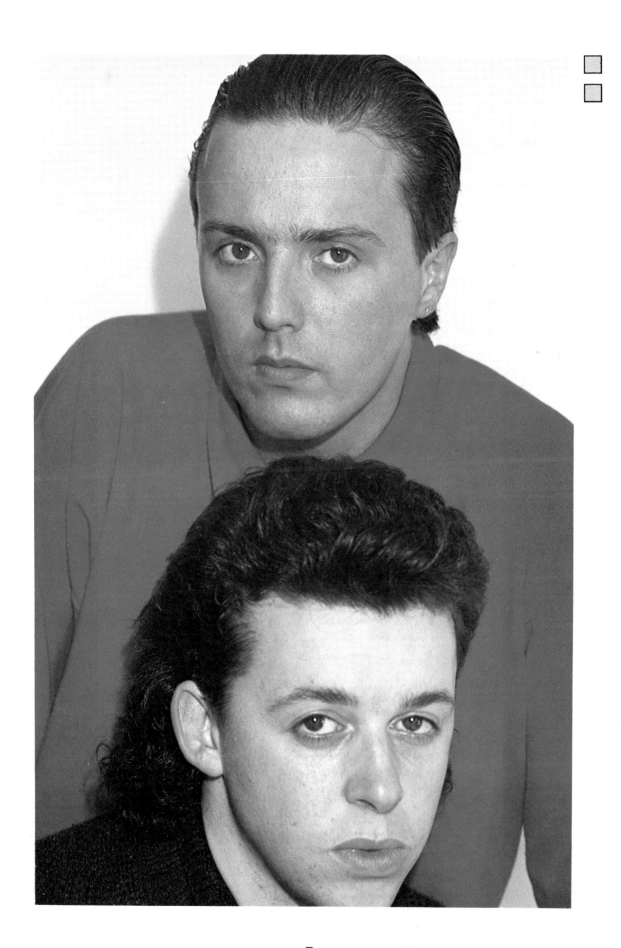

A year after Graduate broke up, Curt was to tell *Sounds:* "I don't understand how *groups* can honestly get on together, how five people with five different ideas can actually operate together, because no set of persons' ideas will ever be the same. I mean, Roland and I think quite closely, but even our ideas aren't exactly the same." The idea of putting together a new group was swiftly discarded and instead Roland and Curt decided to operate as a duo.

1981 had seen a major resurgence in just that format. Soft Cell had just taken their first tentative steps into the big time – and been rewarded with one of the biggest hits of the year, "Tainted Love". Dave Stewart and Barbara Gaskin had teamed up to top the charts with "It's My Party", Linx were at the peak of their powers and just over the horizon there awaited Yazoo, Blancmange and, albeit on a temporary basis only, Paul McCartney and

Stevie Wonder. Into this climate Curt and Roland sank their energies, recording demos of two of Roland's latest songs, "Pale Shelter" and "Suffer The Children".

The songs saw the pair truly shaking off any ghosts of their past which might have haunted them. David Lord, who owned the tiny Bath studio wherein the songs were recorded, introduced the pair to synthesizers – a move which was to completely alter their musical ideas although, again in the light of the present musical climate, it was to present them with a few new problems as well.

"I do get annoyed that people call us a synthesizer duo," Roland was to complain later. "I'd rather we were known as electronic, because the picture you get with synthesizers is 'wimps on synths.' People think it's just the two of us with backing tapes and we don't want to be associated with that! We think that's just a fad, a fashion, whereas electronics and

synthesizers, as such, they're the future of music."

A tape of the two new songs was circulated around record companies and very swiftly Mercury Records took the bait. The duo were picked up by Dave Bates, the man responsible for both Teardrop Explodes and, later Monsoon. And in November, 1981, Mercury released "Suffer The Children", a newly recorded version of the original demo, and the world was given its first glimpse of Tears For Fears.

Tears for fears was a phrase the pair had picked out of Dr. Arthur Janov's Primal Therapy, a controversial field of psychology which advocates crying as a method of relieving fears and neuroses. John Lennon was perhaps Janov's best known disciple – his "Plastic Ono Band" LP in 1970 was conceived as a direct result of the therapy.

"Primal Therapy," Roland says, "is science. It's got nothing to do with religion.

It's no trip. What you do is – and this sounds like fantasy but it's not when you see it in action – you relive the traumas that have happened to you. Basically it's crying. That's why we call ourselves Tears For Fears.... Our whole image – or non-image – is based around crying for your fears. Some people go to a pub and get drunk. We go to the studio and record a song."

He told *Melody Maker's* Steve Sutherland: "We're not cranks. We're just normal people. It's not that heavy. People say 'Oh, the Primal Scream', but it's not screaming or shouting or anything like that. I know it sounds wet, but that's exactly it. Our society is totally based around the suppression of all our emotions.

"If you see someone crying or shouting in the street, it's either embarrassing or it's all hush-hush and that's stupid because they are basic human needs – more basic

than power or smoking, drinking, millions of things that people accept and find more important."

In an interview with *Sounds'* Johnny Waller, several months later, the pair explained how they were first introduced to Janov's work. "We've got a friend who's in therapy, and she had *The Primal Scream,* Janov's first book," Curt said. She lent it to Roland, who – "didn't feel too good at the time. I was into different kinds of philosophy through doing Literature A-Level – Christian Nihilism, that kind of thing.... I even believed in God, y'know. And after reading *The Primal Scream* I thought 'So that's why I feel so bad.' It just seemed so obvious to me."

But although Primal Therapy had worked for Curt and Roland, they were a long way from attempting to foist their beliefs on to their fans. "We're not saying everyone should have PT," Curt said. "But hopefully what we intend to do through our music is let people know it's not cranky. I mean, our stuff is tuneful and accessible." Nevertheless, Roland was to admit: "The most we can hope for is that people listen to our music and say 'That's the way I feel' – that would be the highest compliment for me, because the only way that music can be of any value, true value, is that it brings up pains."

"Suffer The Children", Tears For Fears' first single, certainly did that. Roland said: "Dreams are a release for kids. If they're allowed to be what they want in the daytime, they won't have to invent horrible monsters in their dreams at night." That was the basic message of "Suffer The Children", and it was one which struck a sympathetic chord within almost everyone who heard it – *Sounds'* Johnny Waller claimed he could write a whole issue of that paper about that one song! – yet, saleswise, the single did nothing.

Curt and Roland, when they signed to Mercury, claim to have had only two complete new songs to their name – those that made up their original demo. So while "Wind", the song which appeared on the flip of the first single, was adequate enough as a B-side, it was no suprise when they announced that the second Tears For Fears single was to be the second song from the demo: "Pale Shelter".

Like its predecessor, "Pale Shelter" was a re-recording of the original version of the song and was produced by one-time member of Gong, Mike Howlett. It was a far more dance-orientated song than "Suffer The Children", as was demonstrated by the club success of the extended 12″ version of A-side. And the club success gave way in turn to chart success – although, as Curt was to remark: "It was popular amongst the clubs and with the DJs and got quite a bit of airplay, but it made no impact whatsoever. It got to 193 in the chart and that was only for one week. We were pretty disappointed!"

The band's record company, however, weren't. Tears For Fears' original record contract had been for two singles only. This was now fulfilled, but the label lost little time in re-signing the duo. And that despite the band's marked reluctance to commit themselves to any real direction, either in interviews or on vinyl. Six months elapsed between the release of "Pale Shelter" and Tears For Fears' third single, "Mad World" – six months in which Roland and Curt had sat back and made a serious re-evaluation of their position in the rock world. Paul Colbert of *Melody Maker* encountered the pair at this time; he wrote: 'Roland and Curt are showing the first signs of an artistic team whose dreams have been brutalised by a money-orientated business.' The result was a string of very superficial interviews, verbal games of table tennis in which any but the most inane question would be neatly batted back by one or other of the duo.

"We've changed an awful lot in our attitude towards the music business," Roland said. "We used to be 'artists' you know, innocent and naive. Now we realise that the music business is a career and is geared towards success and if you're not successful you might as well not be in it, which is pathetic."

Tears For Fears, however, were successful. "Mad World", produced by Chris Hughes (of Adam Ant fame), had finally given them the hit they needed. Entering the chart on October 2, within three weeks it had breached the Top 20; a fortnight later the song was beginning a three week residency at number 3. To which Roland's response was: "At least we're successful with a song we really like. It's pointless doing anything good if no-one knows who you are."

And yet "Mad World" came very close to not being released at all. Roland told *Sounds:* "We didn't think "Mad World" was a hit single. We didn't put it out because we thought it was commercial, we just thought it would make a good radio record, something people might like to hear on the radio. Because the first two singles hadn't done anything the people in the company were trying to nudge us and we were playing a few gigs (augmented by other musicians, Tears For Fears played six

low-key gigs around the country in September). That gave it the initial nudge. It just kept going up each week and by the third week it was in the Top 75. We thought it would probably burn out around number 50. We were quite amazed how long it stayed around."

Equally amazing, Roland was to admit later, was the realisation that Tears For Fears were....a Pop Group! "We never promoted ourselves as people because we didn't feel interesting enough or confident enough or good looking enough to do it," he said – illustrating his point by remarking that the sleeves for the first two Tears For Fears' singles didn't even carry a picture of the band. Until "Mad World" we weren't really a pop group with an image," he continued. *Top Of The Pops* changed that. "For a couple of weeks the record company had been saying to us, 'You might be on *Top Of The Pops* so you better be ready.'

"We didn't know what to do, whether to go on with just two of us or use the group we play with live. We didn't have a clue. We went out the same day we were on, we left rehearsals at *TOTPs* and bought some clothes. Everyone chose virtually the same thing.

"I looked at us in the studios at *TOTPs* and thought 'Bloody hell! We're a pop group! Which was a shock! The first time we got on a stage at *TOTPs* we just stood still and did nothing 'cos we didn't know what to do. I thought 'Jesus Christ, we're gonna look like Echo And The Bunnymen!' I thought 'This is useless.' (But) "Mad World" sold a lot of copies, far more than I imagined. We became a pop band overnight."

And with that came a teenybop appeal which, when the *New Musical Express'* Graham K. Smith broached the subject, took Roland completely by suprise. "I can understand that to a certain extent with Curt being the pin-up, but records don't sell purely because of that," he said — completely overlooking the examples set by every pre/pubescent phenomenon from the Osmonds / Cassidy / Rollers triumvirate on down. "People are ultimately attracted to the music. There are loads of good looking people around who are doing nothing. Our music is the thing that's getting to people."

It was fortunate that Tears For Fears did now have something new — chart success — to talk about, because another subject which had once been so dear to

their hearts was now strictly out of bounds. The principles of Primal Therapy, the theories of Dr Janov. Having truly 'suffered for their Art', having had a very important facet of their personal lives held up for public ridicule by cynical rock critics, having had to sit back whilst one music paper described their records as "The sort you'd never admit to owning so you take them out of their original sleeves and hide them in Bunnymen ones instead"; all this had had its effect.

"We didn't explain things too well," Roland later admitted. "And when you're misquoted as well, the picture painted was quite different from the way it actually is...". The picture painted, of course, was of "Wimps. Spotty sixth form poets. Doomladen bores," as writer Eleanor Levy put it.

"The media really went out of their way to highlight a dull and serious image for us," Curt has said. "We were never doomladen, serious people in the first place. That's what people put on us. When you first start you have to have an angle to sell yourself to the press. Phonogram decided to capitalise on that....

"Our lyrics will always be important, but we don't talk about them as much as

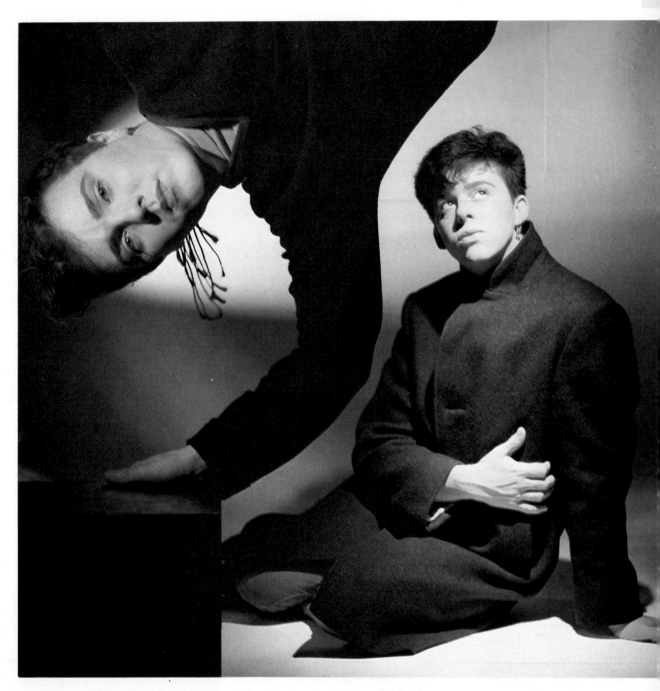

we used to. People say Tears For Fears are a band who write lyrics and make statements. That isn't true because we make music as well and we play live and playing live means entertainment."

Yet playing live was not something the duo particularly enjoyed. Curt told *Sounds*: "I do find it hard playing live. There are so many emotions and you can't put them all across in 45 minutes, and I find it nearly impossible to switch from the emotion of one song to another. I have to

get into the mood of each individual song to be able to perform convincingly and it's virtually impossible to go through all these changes in three quarters of an hour".

It was not a problem which seemed too obvious, though. On October 20, with "Mad World" still charging up the chart, Tears For Fears went out on tour with The Thompson Twins, then a still-struggling cult outfit whose latest single, "Lies", was as transparent an attempt to lure the public *en masse* into the group's camp as

was their titling of the outing "The We're Pop Stars Tour". Transparent, but devastatingly successful. Yet at the time, of the two groups, Tears For Fears were by far the most successful. "Lies" managed to peak at only 67 in the chart – "Mad World", of course, made the Top 3. And the audience at the tour's climax, London Hammersmith Palais, left the impartial observer in very little doubt about which band *should* have been headlining.

With "Mad World" still going strong,

the rush to release a follow-up began. Precision, Graduate's old record company, eventually got in first, taking two songs off the "Acting My Age" album and launching them in the vain hope that as many people as catapulted "Mad World" into the upper echelons of the chart would be aware of Roland and Curt's previous incarnation. They weren't and "Troubled Son" sank as ignominiously as any of its predecessors.

Mercury, too, wanted to get in on the action. Roland claims that he and Curt had already had their next three singles planned long before "Mad World" made the chart; no doubt he had also long decided exactly when each should be released, because much was made in the pages of the music press about a dispute between Tears For Fears and their record company as to whether a new single should be released in time for Christmas. Mercury said 'Yes', Tears For Fears said 'No', nixing even a timely reissue of "Pale Shelter" in favour of waiting until a more superior cut was available. Back in October the band had talked of reissuing the song. "We've re-recorded it and it's come out as it should have done", Curt said – adding that the song would probably be used to open their account in America (a tour was planned for January 1983) because "it sold more there than it did here, and that was on import. It wasn't even released over there".

As it was, the next single was to be "Change", a new song. And it wasn't

released until January – thus avoiding being forced into competition with the likes of Human League, Shakin' Stevens, The Jam and – the Xmas number 1 – Renee and Renato.

"We were against releasing a follow-up to "Mad World" quite so soon because we didn't want to blow out anything it had done. We wanted it to hang around because people don't feel the effects of a hit single until a few months after it's died", Roland said. "So many groups are purely exploitative once they've had hits".

Tears For Fears had no intention of falling into that trap; nevertheless, Curt admitted that "Change" was "more of a step back than a step forward in relation to the direction we'll be going. It's a song we're not particularly happy with, it didn't come out the way we wanted it. We wanted it to be a bit more vibrant. The DJ at our local club won't play the 12" of 'Change'".

Roland, however, had already declared that "the next single should NOT be a departure". While he was more than happy to agree that, with that first all-important hit under their belt Tears For Fears were now in a position whereby they *could* begin releasing more experimental music confident in the knowledge it would reach people simply on the strength of their reputation, he also felt "Change" had been the right choice to make. "It should be a re-affirmation of what's been said previously, and if it says it STRONGER, then it will be even better".

"Change" was an immediate hit, and although its final placing – number 4 for two weeks – was lower than that of "Mad World", sales were at least equal. And it all boded well for the release of the duo's début album "The Hurting" the following month.

Tears For Fears actually began recording the album eight months previous, in July 1982. According to Curt, "It took so long because we were pushed into it before we were ready, before we'd actually established what we wanted to do. The (other) problem was when we looked back at tracks we'd done months before we'd think, 'ooh, I don't like that".

"That's the trouble with technology as well", Roland added. "The more things you pick up the easier it is for you to put down your ideas and now we think if only we'd had this then it would have been a lot easier.

"The album was well on its way for quite some time, but for the past few months we've been regrouping on things that we weren't happy with. It's taken a

long time and cost a lot of money because we're fussy and slightly confused, but the more we go on the less confused we seem to get".

The length of time the album took had another disconcerting result — for its audience if not for the band. The sheer diversity of the material was immense, as *Sounds* pointed out. Weren't the band in danger of confusing people by displaying so many different sides to their music? Curt didn't think so. "It isn't really aimed at anyone in particular — with the hit singles ("The Hurting" included all 4 singles to date, plus 2 B-sides) people will hopefully pick up on it anyway. I think it will appeal to a lot of different people for a lot of different reasons. Hopefully it will trigger people into thinking about it a bit".

Talk of the album's diversity — and with it, the duo's versatility — led to a discussion of their audience. According to Curt: "At gigs you'll get the little girls at the front, the Joy Division fans at the back and even the hippies will put in an appearance. I think it's because we can't be put in a category and consequently neither can our music. If we could be put in a category as people then we'd only appeal to one type of person".

"The Hurting" was an immediate smash. It burst into the Top 20 at number two, the next week it was number one. And while it stayed at the top for just one week, the LP remained on the chart for another four months. When the *New Musical Express* published its annual chart survey, compiled by awarding points for each week a record stayed in the chart, "The Hurting" weighed in at number 12 — behind "Thriller", David Bowie and Wham, but well ahead of Culture Club, Thompson Twins and The Police.

On March 17, the band opened their first major British tour. 23 dates were spread over 27 nights — all sold out well in advance, and were well received by fans and critics alike. *Smash Hits'* reviewer was not alone when he said of the London Lyceum show: "I went home wondering why — when their music is often criticised for being doom-laden — I saw nothing but smiles as I left the ballroom". For Tears For Fears' show, far from being some mournful recital of abject misery and personal neuroses, was a celebration, both musically

and – for Curt and Roland – personally. Their feelings towards live work had changed dramatically in recent months. Now Curt was to say of his previous distaste: "It was purely the fear of not being able to put it across live. After working in a studio for so long you begin to worry if you can actually recreate that sound live. It seems we can though, so it should be quite enjoyable".

"Pale Shelter" was reissued at the end of the tour, taking immediate advantage of

the band's current commercial status by racing up to number 5 in the chart. The following month a three track video tape was released; "Tears For Fears – The Videosingles" featured "Mad World", "Change" and "Pale Shelter", and quickly established itself in the best sellers lists.

But if Tears For Fears were beginning to think they had finally arrived – and who, after three Top 5 singles and a number 1 LP would think anything else? – 1983 was to go out on a very disappointing note,

saleswise at least. After spending almost six months in the studio, apparently working on just the two songs, Tears For Fears released "The Way You Are"/ "Marauders" – their most experimental single to date, and their first not to reach the Top 20 in well over a year. "The Way You Are" reached a mere number 24, prompting *Record Collector's* Richard Jackson to remark, 18 months later, how telling it was that Mercury hadn't even bothered to release a picture disc to accompany the standard 7" and 12" singles ("Pale Shelter" had certainly benefited from this kind of marketing).

An 18 date British tour, featuring two nights in London and winding up in Poole two nights before Christmas, went some way towards healing the duo's bruises, especially as they, themselves, finally felt that they were able to put on the kind of show their audience – and their music – really deserved. Sporadic live work outside Britain had given Tears For Fears a vast

amount of experience, so much so that Roland was to remark of previous British tours: "To be honest we didn't have a CLUE what we were doing then. We had no intention of being entertaining, but were naive enough to think we could just walk on stage and play our songs. The idea backfired. This time there'll be no backing tapes, just seven of us on stage. Because apart from all the trouble you can have with tapes that start running at the wrong speed, I think the public feels it's being conned".

Certainly the group's new show did sound more natural, less reliant on studio trickery than earlier performances, and indeed far truer to something Curt had said back around the time of the first headlining tour. He told *Sounds:* "The beauty of live work is that you've got an hour to do it and you can't go back and change it. It's there, that's the impression people get of you, I think *that's* exciting".

Eight months were to pass between that tour and Tears For Fears' next bout of public appearances; eight months in which they began work on their second LP and — according to Curt — were warned over and

over again by their record company that, if the record wasn't in the shops by the end of July, their career would be over and done with. The public would get bored, the group were assured; fifteen month gaps between LPs might be all right for Fleetwood Mac and The Police, but Tears For Fears were hardly at *that* level, were they?

"That sort of attitude does tend to irritate us a little", Curt told *Melody Maker's* Helen Fitzgerald when the subject of Tears For Fears' lack of "high profile success" was broached. "But then as long as our records keep selling consistently and charting then I don't think that we're that worried. In a sense I feel sorry for bands like Duran who have little or no time to themselves, everybody wants a slice of them. Roland and I couldn't live our lives like that. And with our existing level of success we are allowed to change and progress without having all the associated pressures".

And change, as Ms. Fitzgerald was to observe, was definitely the order of the day. Dismissing Mercury's bleatings, Tears For Fears allowed the "crucial" last day of

July to slip past weeks before releasing even a single; that was "Mother's Talk" – "an anti-nuclear song, written specifically for our friend Maggie", revealed Curt, directly contradicting the critics who had glanced at the title and instantly dug out their old Primal Scream theories again.

"The basic idea for the lyric started from an old wives' tale, the one that says if you pull a face and the wind changes, the face will stay there". The American Cruise missiles which had recently found their way on to British soil were drawn in to complete the analogy – "so it's hinting more towards uglier things". And Primal Therapy? "If people want to know about Primal Therapy they can go and find out about it themselves. It's not for us to preach".

The lyrics might have been interesting, but what most people really wanted to know was; why the sudden change in musical style? After the muted melodies of "The Hurting" and its attendant singles,

"Mother's Talk" was raging, screaming; one paper summed it up as "Heavy drums, loud guitar and football chant vocals". And according to Curt and Roland, it was a taster for a new musical direction....

"We used to be on the Planet Sylvian and now we're on the Planet Rock 'n' Roll", Roland explained. "It's just that the rocket took a long time getting there.

"Rock 'n' Roll, was a dirty word for us before, which is ludicrous. It's exactly what we're doing now. 'Mother's Talk' has got a very basic excitement in it which was lacking in our earlier work. Some of 'The Hurting' was 6th form poetry stuff, I suppose. But now we've taken the darker, stronger stuff which was already there, but everyone ignored, and made it more commercial".

And the first casualty of this new found direction was..."Mother's Talk". The original recording of the song, cut, apparently, in the same mould as its predecessors, was scrapped. In its place

came the version which was ultimately released; punchy, rocking, loud.

"Both of us felt there was something lacking, but we couldn't see our way to breaking away from it. It was a classic case of not being able to see the wood for the trees", Curt said.

So he and Roland took three months off from recording and just concentrated on experimenting in the studio, trying to break out of the mould which they felt had been created by "concentrating too much on things that didn't matter. Our sound was very laid-back before. It wasn't a positive statement and was more easily accessible to anyone. Now it's got more bite to it, more vibrancy. It made us sit up rather than sitting back trying to fit into the 'Hit' formula".

Not that that stopped "Mother's Talk" from making an instant bee-line for the Top 20, coming to rest at number 14; not quite as convincing a chart performance as, say, "Mad World", but still a respectable

blamed producer Chris Hughes for the new influence. "I had lots of artistic tantrums and didn't want to make any money. Then I got a gas bill".

On a more serious note, he continued: "The approach of 'This is going to be big' was healthy. It made the music communicate. We didn't go up our arses – well maybe once. We aren't precious any more, (although) the only reason we were precious is because we were terrible. Now we're going to do things more quickly, make mistakes and make complete prats of ourselves".

Curt said: "When we recorded 'The Hurting' we were very precious and over-indulgent. It got to the point where we didn't want to put anything on tape. There was so much indecision – married with a lack of vision. Everything had to be dead right and consequently we got a lot of things wrong".

"It's all part of growing up. We've become adults", Roland added. "I even shaved yesterday – in certain places".

"Songs From The Big Chair" had only eight songs on it; two previous singles and,

pegging for a band who'd been away for eight months and then come back sounding totally different from before. But in case anybody did have any doubts as to Tears For Fears' ability to reinstate themselves as a major power in the land, they had an ace up their sleeves which was to silence their doubters forever. "Shout" was released in November. According to Curt it was a protest song, "having a go at people who just blindly accept things"; according to *Smash Hits'* singles columnist it was an "altogether more relaxed and accomplished effort than 'Mother's Talk'...effective and powerful Pop with an insidious chorus that you'll find yourself singing at the most inopportune moments". And for that reason, the review concluded, it would be a hit.

And it was. The week before Christmas, "Shout" broke into the Top 20 at number 13. Three weeks later it was at number 4, making it the band's most successful single in over a year. And on March 1st 1985, Tears For Fears finally compounded the promise which had been building for so long when they released "Songs From The Big Chair", their second LP.

Curt thought of the title. It came from "a brilliant, but really disturbing film called *Sybil* – a true story about a girl with sixteen personalities. The big chair is the place where she feels safe, without the threat of other people. Likewise the album's saying what WE want to say. We don't care what other people think about it".

Yet at the same time, Roland admits that the ultimate strategy was to make music that would sell a lot of LPs. He

at the time of writing, two later ones. "Everybody Wants To Rule The World" was the first to appear after the LP had been released (to instant chart-topping status); it, too, rocketed up the chart. It entered at number 5; a fortnight later it was at number 2. And in the USA it gave them their first ever number one – just as they had planned all along. Said Roland: "We did the song to have an American hit. It's got the right beat and feel. If you've got the talent to do that, why not do it? It turns people on to other songs that they might not otherwise hear. And it's still a classic single".

A 27 date British tour was set up, its four well over-subscribed London dates amply testifying to the immensity of Tears For Fears' support – as if anybody needed any further conviction. A week before the tour opened, Mercury announced that "Songs From The Big Chair" had already outsold "The Hurting". And it had only been in the shops a fortnight! Even the enforced cancellation of three nights at the Hammersmith Odeon, brought about by Roland going down with a viral infection and Curt catching 'flu, could not dampen the near-hysteria surrounding the band; instead, the rescheduling of the shows for several months hence only gave the disappointed fans, many of whom also held tickets for the group's Royal Albert Hall show, something else to look forward to.

The two month British tour was only the prelude to a further seven month world tour. At the end of May they set out for the United States, again to a totally overwhelming reception.

Curt had already spent some time in America earlier in the year. While Roland remained at home in Bath, he had flown to Los Angeles to film the desert scenes for the "Everybody Wants To Rule The World" video. Now the pair of them were there, riding high on a wave of national support which, *Melody Maker* reported, took a totally different form to its British counterpart. "While in England Tears For Fears, for all their apparent seriousness, are still not far short of a Teenybop phenomenon, America tends to regard the boys as a more serious proposition altogether", *MM* commented of the band's Boston show. Yet according to Curt: "Our audience has got a lot older. It's all the

over-20s now who sit and listen – they are music lovers rather than just people who come to see you. The letters we receive now are more about the music and why we didn't put a lyric sheet in 'Songs From The Big Chair' than 'I love you, I love you, I want to kiss your bottom.'" Whatever the truth of the matter, there could be little doubt that Tears For Fears, within themselves at least, had arrived at an image (or "non-image", as Roland still liked to remark) which "is going to fit in with what we're doing, rather than the other way around".

"We're not on the defensive any more", Curt told *Melody Maker.* "I used to feel very bitter at the inaccuracies of some of

the criticism (we used to get). I couldn't believe they were talking about me. Now it's more a case of 'This is me, suckers!' — and if they don't like it they can lump it. I'm enjoying myself too much to sit in a corner and worry about being misunderstood. I just wish we could have come to this conclusion ages ago!

"Frankie Goes To Hollywood have this thing of bringing out a different mix every week. Well, we're going to have a different haircut every week...whereas Wham! have a different nose-job every week".

The fourth single from "Songs From The Big Chair", "Head Over Heels", was released midway through June, 1985. It

was, Curt claimed, "The nearest we'll ever get to writing a love song. We don't need to do that, we've got enough romance at home (both he and Roland are married) not to have to write songs about it. It's private, I suppose". It was also another hit, making it as far as number 12 in July. In America, "Everybody Wants To Rule The

World" was still holding steady in the Top 5, while on both sides of the Atlantic, "Songs From The Big Chair" was still fighting off challenges from even media megastars such as Bruce Springsteen and Prince, *et al*, as it dominated the album scene for the third consecutive month.

But even with all this achieved, Tears For Fears were not resting on their laurels. "This year's going to be a gruelling one. But it's also dedicated to having fun", Curt told Melody Maker. In another interview, on the other side of the world, Roland acknowledged what Tears For Fears had achieved so far. And how. "We've succeeded because of good songs, not because we've discovered a new way of wearing clothes or anything. What we're doing is a lot of people's dream, but it's never been a dream for us. It's good, the success, and it's justified, but I don't care about maintaining it even though I know we could, if we set our minds on it, be the biggest band in the world".

Midway through 1985, it looks as if they might not have any say in the matter.

TEARS FOR FEARS DISCOGRAPHY

GRADUATE: singles

3/80:	Elvis Should Play Ska/Julie Julie	Precision PAR 100
5/80:	Ever Met A Day?/Shut Up	Precision PAR 104
10/80:	Ambition/Bad Dreams	Precision PAR 111
3/81:	Shut Up/Ever Met A Day?	Precision PAR 117
12/82:	Troubled Son/Return	Graduate GRAD 1

GRADUATE: album

5/80:	ACTING MY AGE	Precision PART 001

TEARS FOR FEARS: singles

11/81:	Suffer The Children/Wind	Mercury IDEA 1
11/81:	Suffer The Children/instrumental/Wind	Mercury IDEA 12
3/82:	Pale Shelter/The Prisoner	Mercury IDEA 2/2 12
9/82:	Mad World/Ideas As Opiates	Mercury IDEA 3
9/82:	Mad World/Ideas As Opiates/Saxophones...	Mercury IDEA 3 12
1/83:	Change/The Conflict	Mercury IDEA 4/4 12
4/83:	Pale Shelter/We Are Broken	Mercury IDEA 5
4/83:	Pale Shelter/Instrumental/We Are Broken	Mercury IDEA 5 12
11/83:	The Way You Are/Marauders	Mercury IDEA 6/6 12
8/84:	Mother's Talk/Empire Building	Mercury IDEA 7/7 12
9/84:	Mother's Talk (drum mix)/Empire Building	Mercury IDEA 7
11/84:	Shout/The Big Chair	Mercury IDEA 8/8 10
11/84:	Shout/extended mix/The Big Chair	Mercury IDEA 8 12
3/85:	Everybody Wants To Rule The World/Pharaohs	Mercury IDEA 9/9 10
3/85:	Everybody Wants To Rule The World/Pharaohs	Mercury IDEA 9 12
3/85:	as above + Everybody Wants To Rule (urban mix)/Interview	Mercury IDEA 99
6/85:	Head Over Heels/	Mercury IDEA 10

TEARS FOR FEARS: album

3/83:	THE HURTING	Mercury MERS 17
2/85:	SONGS FROM THE BIG CHAIR	Mercury MERH 58